# SCHOLASTIC

# READ & RESPOND

## Bringing the best books to life in the classroom

**Activities based on Stormbreaker**

By Anthony Horowitz

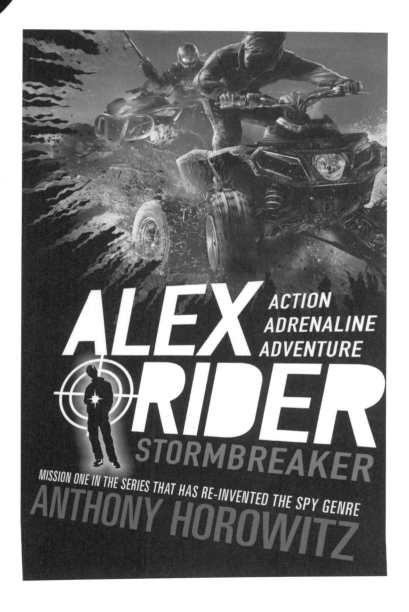

ACTION
ADRENALINE
ADVENTURE

ALEX RIDER
STORMBREAKER

MISSION ONE IN THE SERIES THAT HAS RE-INVENTED THE SPY GENRE

ANTHONY HOROWITZ

# FOR AGES 7–11

Scholastic Education, an imprint of Scholastic Ltd
Book End, Range Road, Witney, Oxfordshire, OX29 0YD
Registered office: Westfield Road, Southam, Warwickshire CV47 0RA

Printed and bound by Ashford Colour Press
© 2018 Scholastic Ltd
1 2 3 4 5 6 7 8 9   8 9 0 1 2 3 4 5 67

British Library Cataloguing-in-Publication Data
A catalogue record for this book is available from the British Library.
ISBN 978-1407-17510-2

Extracts from *The National Curriculum in England, English Programme of Study* © Crown Copyright. Reproduced under the terms of the Open Government Licence (OGL). http://www.nationalarchives.gov.uk/doc/open-government-licence/version/3

Due to the nature of the web, we cannot guarantee the content or links of any site mentioned. We strongly recommend that teachers check websites before using them in the classroom.

**Authors** Sally Burt and Debbie Ridgard
**Editorial team** Audrey Stokes, Vicki Yates, Helen Foster, Suzanne Adams
**Series designers** Neil Salt and Alice Duggan
**Designer** Alice Duggan
**Illustrator** Dave Smith/Beehive Illustration

**Acknowledgements**
The publishers gratefully acknowledge permission to reproduce the following copyright material:
Walker Books Ltd, London SE11 5HJ (www.walker.co.uk) for the use of the cover and extract text from *Stormbreaker* by Antony Horowitz. Text © 2000 Stormbreaker Productions. Alex Rider™ © 2000-2005 Stormbreaker Productions Ltd.

Every effort has been made to trace copyright holders for the works reproduced in this book, and the publishers apologise for any inadvertent omissions.

# CONTENTS

# How to use Read & Respond in your classroom...

Read & Respond provides teaching ideas related to a specific well-loved children's book. Each Read & Respond book is divided into the following sections:

**ABOUT THE BOOK AND AUTHOR**

Gives you some background information about the book and the author.

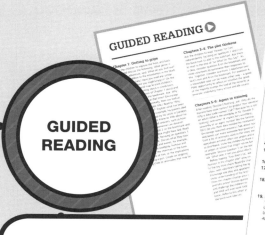

**GUIDED READING**

Breaks the book down into sections and gives notes for using it with guided reading groups. A bookmark has been provided on page 12 containing comprehension questions. The children can be directed to refer to these as they read.

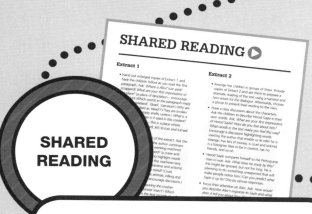

**SHARED READING**

Provides extracts from the children's book with associated notes for focused work. There is also one non-fiction extract that relates to the children's book.

**GRAMMAR, PUNCTUATION & SPELLING**

Provides word-level work related to the children's book so you can teach grammar, punctuation and spelling in context.

## PLOT, CHARACTER & SETTING

Contains activity ideas focused on the plot, characters and the setting of the story.

## GET WRITING

Provides writing activities related to the children's book. These activities may be based directly on the children's book or be broadly based on the themes and concepts of the story.

## TALK ABOUT IT

Has speaking and listening activities related to the children's book. These activities may be based directly on the children's book or be broadly based on the themes and concepts of the story.

## ASSESSMENT

Contains short activities that will help you assess whether the children have understood concepts and curriculum objectives. They are designed to be informal activities to feed into your planning.

> **❝** The titles are great fun to use and cover exactly the range of books that children most want to read. It makes it easy to explore texts fully and ensure the children want to keep on reading more. **❞**
>
> *Chris Flanagan, Year 5 Teacher,*
> *St Thomas of Canterbury*
> *Primary School*

# Activities

The activities follow the same format:

- **Objective:** the objective for the lesson. It will be based upon a curriculum objective, but will often be more specific to the focus being covered.

- **What you need:** a list of resources you need to teach the lesson, including printable pages.

- **What to do:** the activity notes.

- **Differentiation:** this is provided where specific and useful differentiation advice can be given to support and/or extend the learning in the activity. Differentiation by providing additional adult support has not been included as this will be at a teacher's discretion based upon specific children's needs and ability, as well as the availability of support.

The activities are numbered for reference within each section and should move through the text sequentially – so you can use the lesson while you are reading the book. Once you have read the book, most of the activities can be used in any order you wish.

# CURRICULUM LINKS

| Section | Activity | Curriculum objectives |
| --- | --- | --- |
| **Guided reading** | | Comprehension: To maintain positive attitudes to reading and understanding of what they read. |
| **Shared reading** | 1 | Comprehension: To explore the meaning of words in context; to discuss and evaluate how authors use figurative language, considering the impact on the reader. |
| | 2 | Comprehension: To draw inferences, justifying them with evidence. |
| | 3 | Comprehension: To discuss and evaluate how authors use language, including figurative language, considering the impact on the reader; to identify and discuss themes and conventions in and across a wide range of writing. |
| | 4 | Comprehension: To identify how language, structure and presentation contribute to meaning. |
| **Grammar, punctuation & spelling** | 1 | Transcription: To spell words containing the letter string 'ough'. |
| | 2 | Vocabulary, grammar and punctuation: To use modal verbs...to indicate degrees of possibility. |
| | 3 | Transcription: To spell some words with 'silent' letters. |
| | 4 | Vocabulary, grammar and punctuation: To use dashes to indicate parenthesis. |
| | 5 | Vocabulary, grammar and punctuation: To use semicolons to mark boundaries between independent clauses. |
| | 6 | Vocabulary, grammar and punctuation: To use the perfect form of verbs to mark relationships of time and cause. |
| **Plot, character & setting** | 1 | Composition: In writing narratives, to consider how authors have developed characters. |
| | 2 | Comprehension: To draw inferences such as inferring characters' feelings, thoughts and motives from their actions, justifying inferences with evidence. |
| | 3 | Comprehension: To discuss and evaluate how authors use language, including figurative language, considering the impact on the reader. |
| | 4 | Comprehension: To summarise the main ideas drawn from more than one paragraph, identifying key details that support the main ideas. |
| | 5 | Comprehension: To provide reasoned justifications for their views. |
| | 6 | Comprehension: To explain and discuss their understanding of what they have read. |
| | 7 | Comprehension: To identify and discuss conventions in writing. |
| | 8 | Comprehension: To identify and discuss conventions in writing; to predict what might happen from details stated and implied. |

| Section | Activity | Curriculum objectives |
|---|---|---|
| **Talk about it** | 1 | Spoken language: To speak audibly and fluently with an increasing command of Standard English. |
| | 2 | Spoken language: To gain, maintain and monitor the interest of the listener. |
| | 3 | Spoken language: To participate in...role play. |
| | 4 | Spoken language: To participate in discussions; to articulate and justify...opinions. |
| | 5 | Spoken language: To use spoken language to...imagine and explore ideas. |
| | 6 | Spoken language: To articulate and justify answers...opinions. |
| **Get writing** | 1 | Composition: To identify the audience for and purpose of the writing, selecting the appropriate form and using other similar writing as models for their own. |
| | 2 | Composition: To note and develop initial ideas, drawing on reading...where necessary; to identify the audience for and purpose of the writing. |
| | 3 | Composition: To use...organisational and presentational devices to structure text and to guide the reader. |
| | 4 | Composition: To describe settings, characters and atmosphere and integrate dialogue to convey character and advance the action; to perform their own compositions, using appropriate intonation, volume, and movement so that meaning is clear. |
| | 5 | Composition: Selecting appropriate grammar and vocabulary, understanding how such choices can change and enhance meaning. |
| | 6 | Composition: To identify the audience for and purpose of the writing, selecting the appropriate form and using other similar writing as models for their own. |
| **Assessment** | 1 | Spoken language: To speak audibly and fluently. |
| | 2 | Spoken language: To ask relevant questions to extend their understanding and knowledge. |
| | 3 | Composition: To select appropriate grammar and vocabulary, understanding how such choices can change and enhance meaning. |
| | 4 | Composition: To use...organisational and presentational devices to structure text and to guide the reader. |
| | 5 | Transcription: To use dictionaries to check the spelling and meaning of words; to use a thesaurus. |
| | 6 | Composition: To identify the audience for and purpose of the writing, selecting the appropriate form. |

## Key facts
*Stormbreaker*

◉ **Author:**
Anthony Horowitz

◉ **First published:**
4 September 2000

◉ **Awards:**
Listed on the BBC's 'The Big Read'; Wisconsin Golden Archer Award (2003); Rebecca Caudill Young Reader's Book Award (2004); California Young Reader Medal (2005).

◉ **Adaptations:**
Made into a full-length feature film and a graphic novel.

◉ **Did you know?**
*Stormbreaker* has sold more than nine million copies worldwide.

## About the book

*Stormbreaker* is the first novel in the popular *Alex Rider* series. It is a spy-fiction adventure novel set in modern-day Britain. The main character, Alex Rider, thinks he is an ordinary 14-year-old, who lives with his uncle, Ian Rider. When he receives news of his uncle's death in a car crash, Alex decides to investigate the answers to his mounting questions. He soon discovers his uncle was a spy for Britain's Secret Intelligence Service (MI6), who have decided Alex is the perfect person to finish the job his uncle had started. He is sent on an intense training course in preparation for his mission – to infiltrate Sayle Enterprises and discover what lies behind its doors and its founder, Herod Sayle. Acting as a computer geek, armed with the knowledge from his short training, a couple of hi-tech gadgets and survival skills learned from his uncle, Alex follows the clues his uncle left to save Britain's school kids from catastrophic disaster.

## About the author

Anthony Horowitz is one of Britain's most prolific writers, having written more than 40 novels for children, young adults and adults. He has also written scripts and screenplays for radio, theatre, television and feature films.

He was born on 5 April 1955 in Middlesex, England. After many unhappy years at school, he attended the University of York and graduated with a degree in English Literature and Art History. Although he describes his years at boarding school as 'brutal', they were later a source of inspiration for his stories. He loved reading and writing from an early age and would entertain his friends with Frankenstein and Dracula stories.

*The Sinister Secret of Frederick K Bower*, a children's adventure published in 1979, was followed by the first Pentagram series book, *The Devil's Door-Bell*. He also wrote *Groosham Grange*, *The Diamond Brothers* and *The Power of Five* for adults.

He was asked to write the new Sherlock Holmes novels, *The House of Silk* and, more recently, *Moriarty*. He was also chosen by the Ian Fleming estate to write *Trigger Mortis*, a new James Bond novel.

Anthony Horowitz has created and adapted many stories for television, including *Injustice*, *Collision* and the award-winning *Foyle's War*.

In 2014, he was awarded an OBE for 'Services to Literature'. He lives in London with his wife, Gill Green, and two sons who, he says, help with ideas and research. He is patron of the child's protection charity, Kidscape.

# GUIDED READING ▶

## Chapter 1: Getting to grips

Invite the children to explore the front and back covers and discuss the following: *What genre is it?* (fiction, adventure, spy); *What do you find out?* (Guide the children to the information in the blurb and any other clues.) *Have you read any similar books? Do you think you might enjoy it?* On the board, develop a mind map to track children's responses, before inviting storyline predictions.

Read the first sentence of Chapter 1 aloud and discuss question 15 on the bookmark. Ask: *Why might the doorbell ring at that time?* (Encourage the children to answer generally, then use textual evidence such as the chapter title.) Read to 'Why would the police have lied?' Explore what has been established about Alex (for example, his parents died and he has been brought up by his uncle in London). Ask: *Why do you think Alex knew so little about his uncle?* (Encourage reasoned answers, such as how being familiar or close to someone can diminish curiosity.) Consider question 2 on the bookmark and invite reasons why the police might have lied. Read to the end of the chapter, focusing on questions 1 and 13 on the bookmark. Discuss what they now know about characters and events, for example, about Alex through his wordplay, humour and manner of speaking; the chairman of the bank through descriptions of him; or the implications of the driver having a gun. Create an ongoing wallchart, listing clues or anomalies that may be relevant.

## Chapters 2–4: The plot thickens

Ask the children to read 'Heaven for Cars' independently, focusing on questions 1 and 2 on the bookmark to add to the wallchart. Ask them to read to the end of 'So What Do You Say?'. As a class, consider question 8 on the bookmark and invite volunteers to summarise their responses to this. Together, consider questions 3 (blackmail over Jack's visa) and 4 on the bookmark. For question 4, a reasonable case can be made either way – a good PSHE opportunity to reflect on whether the good of the majority trumps the bad of the minority (a principle underlying many school and life issues).

## Chapters 5–6: Agent in training

After reading 'Double 0 Nothing', ask: *Why do the trainees have code names?* (to protect their identities) *Why is Alex code-named 'Cub'?* (because he is not an adult) *What is the wordplay in his 'Double 0 Nothing' nickname?* (It implies he's worthless, unworthy of an agent number like the famous 007.) *Do you think Alex minded his nickname?* (Encourage reasoned answers.) Talk about how nicknames can make someone feel good or bad. Start a list of acronyms used in the story; explain that specialised activities often use jargon and acronyms as shorthand. Invite the children to think of acronyms or jargon at school that might not be familiar to everyone. Discuss question 5 on the bookmark and ask: *What does it tell you about Alex's character?*

Before reading 'Toys Aren't Us', ask: *What is the humour in the chapter title?* (play on words relating to the toy store chain) Read the chapter to the class, with volunteers taking the speaking parts. Encourage role play and appropriate expression to show understanding of the text and characters. Ask: *Does this chapter change your opinion of Mr Blunt and Mrs Jones?* Discuss question 6 on the bookmark and challenge the children to predict whether Alex and Wolf will ever work together (they do in another book). Refer to this when you consider question 9 on the bookmark later on.

## Chapters 7–9: Undercover operations

Ask the children to read to the end of 'Night Visitors'. In groups, invite them to discuss questions 12 and 14 on the bookmark. They should now be familiar with Alex's dry sense of humour in his quips and quick retorts. His humour distracts from some of the more violent and shocking aspects of the story. Discuss the events in relation to rising action (build-up) and explore the effect of the jellyfish on the atmosphere and mood: it symbolises latent threat. Sayle's description of it and why he feels akin to it are clues to his malevolent rather than benevolent intent. Ask: *Was Alex wise to win the snooker game so resoundingly?* (Probably not. It may have put Sayle more on guard, especially after Alex's name slip and Sayle noting his resemblance to Ian Rider.)

Still working as a class, consider question 13 on the bookmark. Invite the children to share sentences or short extracts they find unusual, effective, humorous or evocative and discuss the techniques employed to create the effect. Begin with an example: 'This was a car that sneered at speed limits.' (personification).

## Chapters 10–12: The stakes rise

Ask the children to read 'Death in the Long Grass' and 'Dozmary Mine' in groups, taking turns to read. Discuss how both chapters heighten the tension and raise the stakes for Alex in different ways. The description of the 'killing field' is vivid and rather shocking, forcing Alex to register the reality of Mrs Jones' words: '...you're never too young to die'. Ask: *What mistakes does Alex believe he's made?* Point out how the tension is intensified by the absence of Alex's dry humour and how attention to detail makes Alex's experience in the mine so realistic. *Was Alex brave or foolhardy? What would you have done?*

Read 'Behind the Door' to the class. This chapter reveals the full extent of the problem confronting Alex and MI6. Invite a volunteer to explain the significance of what Alex sees on the assembly line and its link to Sayle's 'generous' plan. *What will happen if the Prime Minister presses the switch at the Science Museum? What is significant about the launch date?* (It mocks the Prime Minister and the country – 'April fools'.)

## Chapters 15–17: Endgame

Invite the children to predict what happens to Alex, then ask them to read independently to the end of 'Eleven O'Clock'. Ask: *Why was Sayle so bitter?* Encourage them to reflect on the contrast between Sayle's version of his life and how it appears from the outside. Invite volunteers to recall how Alex used Smithers' gadgets. Examine the importance of gadgets in the spy genre, encouraging children to share their prior knowledge of books or films in this genre.

Before reading 'Twelve O'Clock', ask the children to imagine how Alex could save the day using the Bomber Boy cartridge. Read the chapter aloud to where the clock begins to strike. Ask: *What does Sayle really mean in his speech to the Prime Minister? Why doesn't the Prime Minister understand?* (The Prime Minister bullied Sayle at school; Sayle is taking revenge by making the Prime Minister, who doesn't remember school in the same light, directly responsible.)

Before reading the final chapter, reflect together on question 17 on the bookmark (he has been prepared by his life with his uncle; his personality, perseverance, courage, loyalty to Jack). Ask: *What loose ends still need to be resolved?* (MI6's reaction, Sayle's and Yassen's whereabouts, what will happen to Alex) Invite predictions before reading 'Yassen' as a class.

## Characters, setting and themes

One of the author's techniques is attention to detail in describing characters. Re-read extracts where characters first appear, noting how the author uses physical descriptions, quirky comparisons, even names (Mrs Jones – ordinary, unnoticeable name, possibly a cover; Mr Blunt; Mr Crawley; Smithers; Nadia Vole). Ask: *How else does the author develop the characters?* (through their manner of speaking, expressions, actual dialogue, thoughts and actions)

Alex and Sayle are the most developed characters: Alex – the protagonist, the story narrated from his perspective; Sayle – the antagonist, the contrast between how he views his life and how everyone else seems to. The other characters are facilitators to the unfolding events, often neither clearly good nor bad; even Ian Rider lied to Alex while preparing him, seemingly intentionally, for intelligence work. Ask: *Is Yassen Gregorovich Alex's friend or foe?* (He killed Alex's uncle but doesn't kill for killing's sake if not so contracted.) Ask: *Do you think Yassen meant to save Alex when killing Sayle?* (Encourage children to use textual evidence.)

The story is set between London and Cornwall, although the Royal and General office and Port Tallon are fictitious. All not being as it seems is a recurrent theme in the book. Alex must question everything he's always taken for granted: he realises he knew little about his uncle and didn't even know what 'Jack' was short for – while he'd wondered occasionally, his curiosity had not prevailed. Once his suspicions are aroused, however, he questions everything. While the story touches on themes such as resourcefulness, loyalty and honour, and trust and survival, it is mostly about Alex trying to make sense of the unpredictable adult world where everyone seems capable of dissembling – even those closest to him. This forces him to rely on and trust himself. End by inviting children to consider question 19 on the bookmark.

## Structure and style

Invite the children to analyse question 10 on the bookmark. Then, ask them to discuss question 16. The book has a third-person narrator who tells the story from Alex's perspective. Ask: *How would the book differ if it were written in first-person narrative?* (There would be no scenes without Alex, no comments other than his.) Encourage children to reflect on question 18 on the bookmark.

The author uses entertaining dialogue to reveal personality, attitudes and motivation. While the narrator usually tells the reader Alex's thoughts, the narrative style tends to be informal and conversational, at times giving the effect of first-person narrative. Encourage the children to enjoy the humour and figurative language in the text. Create a wallchart of favourite comparisons (similes, metaphors, personification) and use of vocabulary.

Ask the children to discuss question 7 on the bookmark and vote on the most exciting cliffhanger. Together, consider question 11 on the bookmark, and share ideas in a plenary session. The book has few illustrations, restricted to maps, notes and signs. Encourage children to see how this frees them to develop their own mental images. Ask whether anyone has seen the film of this book, and analyse whether it is preferable to see the film or read the book first.

The book is the first in a series featuring Alex Rider and his adventures with MI6. Ask the children to consider question 9 on the bookmark. The story contains various clues. In addition, some versions of the cover advertise it as part of a series, and some editions include a trailer for the next book. As a class, share ideas on what is needed for a novel to become a series: strong main character; a scenario that can easily launch further episodes or plots; hints of characters who may reappear in future instalments; loose ends.

## Stormbreaker
### by Anthony Horowitz

### Focus on... Meaning

1. What clues in this chapter set up the plot?
2. What is the significance of Alex's uncle always wearing a seatbelt?
3. Why does Alex agree to his mission?
4. Are Mr Blunt and Mrs Jones good or bad characters?
5. Why does Alex help Wolf with his parachute jump?
6. Predict how Alex's gadgets could be used.

### Focus on... Organisation

7. Which chapter has the most exciting cliffhanger ending?
8. What is Alex's dilemma, and how does it link to the problem to be solved in the story?
9. What indicates the book might be part of a series?
10. Which chapters correspond to these story stages: introduction, build-up, climax, resolution and conclusion?

## Stormbreaker
### by Anthony Horowitz

### Focus on... Language and features

11. Would the book be enhanced if it had more illustrations? Why?
12. What does the dialogue reveal about Alex?
13. Identify examples of the author's techniques to enhance description and evoke images.
14. How does the author use humour in the story?

### Focus on... Purpose, viewpoints and effects

15. How does the first sentence grab your attention?
16. Who narrates the story?
17. What made Alex such a good choice for the mission?
18. How would the story be different if it were told from Herod Sayle's perspective?
19. In what ways could the saying 'Never judge a book by its cover' summarise the message in this book? Can you think of other appropriate sayings?

# SHARED READING ▶

## Extract 1

- Hand out enlarged copies of Extract 1 and have the children follow as you read the first paragraph. Ask: *Where is Alex?* (car yard/ scrapyard) *What are your first impressions of the place?* (a place of desolation – encourage discussion) *Which words in the paragraph imply death?* ('wasteland', 'dead', 'carcasses') *Why are the cars described as 'dead'?* (They are broken beyond repair, empty shells, useless.) *What is a 'wasteland' and how is it used in this context?* (A place without life – this is a place where broken cars are dumped, left to rust and turned into scrap metal.)

- Continue reading the rest of the extract. Ask the children to consider how the author continues the theme of death. *What working machines does Alex see in the scrapyard?* (a crane and a crusher) Ask the children to highlight words in the text used to describe the machines (any words describing their appearance and actions). Ask: *What image comes to mind?* (Cruel, hungry, caged monster-like animals, killing and devouring dead victims – encourage discussion.)

- Ask: *Find the simile comparing the crusher to an animal.* ('like a monster insect') *Which other words/phrases in the text provide clues?* ('roared', 'metal claw', 'scoop up...carry it away', 'seized it in a metallic grip', 'belch', 'wings')

- Consider the yard. Ask: *How can you tell that visitors are not welcome?* (There's a high brick wall with razor wire to keep people out, a security guard, and Alex must avoid being seen.) *What does it remind you of?* (a jail)

## Extract 2

- Arrange the children in groups of three. Provide copies of Extract 2 and ask them to prepare a dramatic reading of the text using a narrator and two voices for the dialogue. Afterwards, choose a group to present their reading to the class.

- Have a class discussion about the characters. Ask the children to describe Herod Sayle in their own words. Ask: *What are your first impressions of Herod Sayle? How do you feel about him? What words in the text make you feel this way?* Encourage a discussion highlighting words used by the author that enable us to infer he is strange, has lots of money, is cruel and unkind, is a foreigner, likes to be in control, has no friends, and so on.

- Herod Sayle compares himself to the Portuguese man-o'-war. Ask: *What does he imply by this?* (He might be ignored, but not for long. He is planning to do something unexpected that will make people notice him.) *Can you predict what Sayle is up to?* Discuss various responses.

- Focus their attention on Alex. Ask: *How would you describe Alex's response to Sayle and what does it tell you about how Alex feels towards him?* (honest/blunt, seemingly innocent yet he has his own motives, suspicious, careless, brave, outspoken, disagreeable, not intimidated)

## Extract 3

- Arrange the children in pairs. Hand out copies of Extract 3 and ask them to take turns reading it aloud to their partner.

- Ask: *How did you feel when reading the text?* (Readers should have sensed Alex's desperation and need for air – encourage discussion.) Describe the tone and pace of the text (urgent, serious, life-threatening). *What textual clues are there to help the reader with expression?* (punctuation marks, short sentences, repetition of words, italics, short questions)

- Look at the words 'Pull, kick'. Ask: *What is the effect of the repetition and then the change when the words are separated?* (Initially the repetition of the single words implies a quick, determined pace. When Alex's strength wavers, the author separates the words with 'and' to show a weakening or slowing down of the action.)

- Consider the descriptive images. *What was the cold water to Alex?* ('a hammer blow') *Explain the effect of the metaphor.* (It describes how jarring and possibly painful the cold was for Alex.) *Have you ever experienced cold water to this degree? Explain how 'The freezing cold was sucking the strength out of him.'* ('Sucking' is a figurative image. Alex felt increasingly cold and weak and unable to move.) Discuss the effect of the figurative images 'a black, swirling, freezing version of hell' and 'A silent scream exploded inside him'.

- Ask children to identify the longest sentence in the extract ('And then the rope tilted upwards…') and explain its effect (it expresses Alex's sense of relief and ability to breathe again).

## Extract 4

- Hand out copies of the extract and ask the children to skim the text. Ask: *Do you think the extract is fact or fiction? Why?* (factual/information text – contains facts about the topic and uses scientific vocabulary) *What layout devices are used to structure the text?* (main heading, subheadings, labelled diagram, bullet points, text box, bold text, colons) *Is the language formal or informal?* (formal) Ask the children to highlight words that are challenging to read. Discuss pronunciation and meaning.

- Ask two volunteers to take turns reading the extract aloud as the rest of the class follows.

- Discuss the layout. Ask: *What is the purpose of the bullet points?* (to organise the text and introduce information) *What is the purpose of the text box?* (to organise the text, make it easier for the reader, improve the layout, highlight certain information)

- Pose questions to check comprehension. *Where does the common name 'man-o'-war' come from?* (It resembles an old sailing battleship.) *Why is it called a 'floating terror'?* (It is a dangerous, floating sea creature.) *How many organisms does it comprise?* (four) *Why should you be careful of a washed-up tentacle?* (It can still sting.) *What is a carnivore?* (a meat-eater)

- With a partner, invite children to go through the text and highlight the key words. Remind them to focus on important nouns, verbs and adjectives. Let them work in pairs to draw a mind map and add the key words. Re-group and share their ideas with the class.

# Extract 1

J.B. Stryker's was a square of wasteland behind the railway tracks running out of Waterloo Station. The area was enclosed by a high brick wall topped with broken glass and razor wire. Two wooden gates hung open, and from the other side of the road Alex could see a shed with a security window and beyond it the tottering piles of dead and broken cars. Everything of any value had been stripped away and only the rusting carcasses remained, heaped one on top of the other, waiting to be fed into the crusher.

There was a guard sitting in the shed, reading the *Sun*. In the distance, a crane coughed into life, then roared down on a battered Ford Mondeo, its metal claw smashing through the window to scoop up the vehicle and carry it away. A phone rang somewhere in the shed and the guard turned round to answer it. That was enough for Alex. Holding his bike and wheeling it along beside him, he sprinted through the gates.

He found himself surrounded by dirt and debris. The smell of diesel was thick in the air and the roar of the engines was deafening. Alex watched as the crane swooped down on another of the cars, seized it in a metallic grip and dropped it into a crusher. For a moment the car rested on a pair of shelves. Then the shelves lifted up, toppling the car over and down into a trough. The operator – sitting in a glass cabin at one end of the crusher – pressed a button and there was a great belch of black smoke. The shelves closed in on the car like a monster insect folding in its wings. There was a grinding sound as the car was crushed until it was no bigger than a rolled-up carpet. Then the operator threw a gear and the car was squeezed out, metallic toothpaste being chopped up by a hidden blade. The slices tumbled on to the ground.

# Extract 2

Herod Sayle was short. He was so short that Alex's first impression was that he was looking at a reflection that had somehow been distorted. In his immaculate and expensive black suit, with gold signet-ring and brightly polished black shoes, he looked like a scaled-down model of a multi-millionaire businessman. His skin was very dark, so that his teeth flashed when he smiled. He had a round, bald head and very horrible eyes. The grey irises were too small, completely surrounded by white. Alex was reminded of tadpoles before they hatch. When Sayle stood next to him, the eyes were almost at the same level as his and held less warmth than the jellyfish.

"The Portuguese man-o'-war," Sayle continued. He had a heavy accent brought with him from the Beirut marketplace. "It's beautiful, don't you think?"

"I wouldn't keep one as a pet," Alex said.

"I came upon this one when I was diving in the South China Sea." Sayle gestured at a glass display case and Alex noticed three harpoon guns and a collection of knives resting in velvet slots. "I love to kill fish," Sayle went on. "But when I saw this specimen of *Physalia physalis*, I knew I had to capture it and keep it. You see, it reminds me of myself."

"It's ninety-nine per cent water. It has no brain, no guts and no anus." Alex had dredged up the facts from somewhere and spoken them before he knew what he was doing.

Sayle glanced at him, then turned back to the creature hovering over him in its tank. "It's an outsider," he said. "It drifts on its own, ignored by the other fish. It is silent and yet it demands respect. You see the nematocysts, Mr Lester? The stinging cells? If you were to find yourself wrapped in those, it would be an exquisite death."

"Call me Alex," Alex said.

# Extract 3

The cold was ferocious, a hammer blow that nearly forced the air out of his lungs. The water pounded at his head, swirling round his nose and eyes. His fingers were instantly numb. His whole system felt the shock, but the dry suit was holding, sealing in at least some of his body warmth. Clinging to the rope, he kicked forward. He had committed himself. There could be no going back.

Pull, kick. Pull, kick. Alex had been underwater for less than a minute but already his lungs were feeling the strain. The roof of the tunnel was scraping his shoulders and he was afraid that it would tear through the dry suit and gouge his skin as well. But he didn't dare slow down. The freezing cold was sucking the strength out of him. Pull and kick. Pull and kick. How long had he been under? Ninety seconds? A hundred? His eyes were tight shut, but if he opened them there would be no difference. He was in a black, swirling, freezing version of hell. And his breath was running out.

He pulled himself forward along the rope, burning the skin off the palms of his hands. He must have been swimming for almost two minutes. It felt closer to ten. He *had* to open his mouth and breathe, even if it was water that would rush into his throat... A silent scream exploded inside him. Pull, kick. Pull, kick. And then the rope tilted upwards and he felt his shoulders come clear, and his mouth was wrenched open in a great gasp as he breathed air and knew that he had made it, perhaps with only seconds to spare.

But made it to where?

Alex couldn't see anything. He was floating in utter darkness, unable to see even where the water ended.

# Extract 4

## FACT FILE: PHYSALIA PHYSALIS

The Atlantic Portuguese man-o'-war is often mistaken for a jellyfish. However, 'it' is actually a 'they', since it is a colony of four individual organisms, called polyps, all working together.

crest

pneumatophore

gastrozooids and gonozooids

tentacles

- **The pneumatophore:** The uppermost organism is a gas-filled bladder which sits on the water. It is said to resemble sailing battleships of old. When threatened, it can deflate its airbag and briefly submerge.

- **The tentacles:** The tentacles are a separate organism extending 9–50 metres. They are covered in venomous stinging cells, nematocysts, that paralyse and kill its prey. A detached tentacle can still inflict a severe sting.

- **The gastrozooids:** They are responsible for digestion.

- **The gonozooids:** They are responsible for reproduction.

Bluebottles float on warm ocean waters, drifting in groups of up to 1000. They are carnivores that feed on fish, squid, plankton and small crustaceans. Their sting is extremely painful causing welts that last 2–3 days.

**Scientific classification**

**Kingdom:** Animalia

**Phylum:** Cnidaria

**Class:** Hydrozoa

**Order:** Siphonophora

**Family:** Physaliidae

**Genus:** Physalia

**Species:** physalis

**Common names:** Portuguese man-o'-war; bluebottle; floating terror

# GRAMMAR, PUNCTUATION & SPELLING ▶

## 1. Spelling 'ough' is tough!

> **Objective**
> To spell words containing the letter string 'ough'.
>
> **What you need**
> Copies of *Stormbreaker*, photocopiable page 22 'Spelling 'ough' is tough'.

### What to do

- Write the letter string 'ough' in the centre of the board. Ask pairs to generate words containing this letter string. Begin with some examples such as 'thought' and 'rough'. After a few minutes, bring the class together and build a mind map on the board of the words they suggest. Add any others they haven't thought of. Discuss and categorise the words on the mind map according to the sounds made by the 'ough' letter string ('oo'; 'uff'; 'or'; long 'o' (as in flow); short 'u' (as in cup); 'off').

- Enhance the children's awareness of the letter string in a number of ways: practising writing it to activate motor memory; differentiating the different sounds it can make to associate them with the letter string; encouraging visual memory by looking out for 'ough' words while reading; and seeing the words in context, particularly the homophones ('bough'/'bow', 'through'/'threw', 'sought'/'sort', 'fought'/'fort') or easily confused words ('cough'/'cuff'). Keep an 'ough' wallchart with page references from the book, including definitions and similar-sounding words.

- Hand out photocopiable page 22 'Spelling 'ough' is tough' for children to complete independently.

> **Differentiation**
> **Support:** Children can practise writing each word to entrench motor memory.
>
> **Extension:** Children can find other words containing the 'ough' sounds, underlining the different letter strings making the same sound.

## 2. Would it or could it?

> **Objective**
> To use modal verbs to indicate degrees of possibility.
>
> **What you need**
> Copies of *Stormbreaker*.

### What to do

- Revise auxiliary/helping verbs. *Which verbs act as auxiliary verbs to form verb tenses?* ('to be' and 'to have') Invite the children to give examples of verbs in the past, future or continuous tenses. Write some of these on the board and discuss the verb components: auxiliary (in different tenses) + participle (past or present).

- Explain that modal verbs are also auxiliary verbs. They change or affect other verbs in a sentence, but cannot act alone – they appear with the infinitive verb (not a participle). Write the main modals on the board: 'might', 'may', 'must', 'should', 'would', 'could', 'can', 'will' and 'shall'. Invite volunteers to use them in sentences and discuss their effect. Primarily, they indicate levels of possibility or ability, show obligation or grant permission. Discuss the difference between 'must', 'may', 'might' and 'will', and then 'should' and 'could', again inviting example sentences.

- Ask the children to read the chapter 'Dozmary Mine' in groups, and to note examples of modal verbs. Among other things, Alex wonders what will, could or would happen, weighing up the possibilities. Now, ask them to create five sentences as Alex, using different modal verbs to say what could/would/should/must/may or might happen next. Share ideas in a plenary session.

> **Differentiation**
> **Support:** Give children sentences with a space to add a sensible modal.
>
> **Extension:** Challenge children to use modals in questions or in the negative form.

## 3. Silent but deadly

**Objective**

To spell some words with 'silent' letters.

**What you need**

Dictionaries, copies of *Stormbreaker*.

### What to do

- Divide the board into three columns, with headings 'beginning', 'middle' and 'end'. In each column, write an example word with a silent letter ('wring', 'reign', 'comb'), underlining the silent letter. Invite volunteers to suggest other words with silent letters until you have identified the common silent letters: 'b', 'c', 'g', 'h', 'k', 'l', 'n', 'p', 't', 'u', 'w'. Discuss where the silent letter usually appears in a word – some can appear in more than one place (for example, 'gnash', 'sign'; 'wreck', 'awry').

- Explain that many English words originate in languages like French, Latin, Greek, German and Old English, which over time has led to the silent letters in English spelling.

- Ask pairs of children to choose one or two silent letters and to find words in the book containing these. They must write each word on a separate sticky note with the silent letter in a different colour. Bring the class together and create a display of words with silent letters, categorised either by letter or by position in the word. Regularly hold mini-challenges: hold up a silent letter and ask the children to write down words with that silent letter.

**Differentiation**

**Support:** Allocate pairs silent letters at the beginning of words so they can use dictionaries to help them.

**Extension:** Ask children to make a wallchart of silent-letter words that are also homophones.

## 4. Dash it!

**Objective**

To use dashes to indicate parenthesis.

**What you need**

Copies of *Stormbreaker*, photocopiable page 23 'Dash!'

### What to do

- Read 'Death in the Long Grass' and ask: *How are hyphens and dashes different?* (hyphens: short, no space either side; dashes: longer, space either side, single or in pairs) Invite volunteers to explain the function of each, using examples from the chapter (hyphen: create compound words and avoid ambiguity; dash: add extra information to the main sentence) Note: some editions may use hyphens to split words at the end of a line. Explain this helps typeset words that don't fit on the line; it's not a grammatical function.

- Re-read the paragraphs where Alex first hears an engine sound and use these to clarify the function of dashes. Ask: *Why are dashes sometimes used in pairs and sometimes singly?* (in pairs: brackets/parenthesis; singly: add an afterthought or additional information) *What punctuation could replace the pairs of dashes?* (commas or brackets) *Why do you think dashes are used to indicate parenthesis in this book more than commas or brackets?* (In general, dashes are less formal than brackets or commas. They fit well with the book's narrative style, echoing how Alex speaks and thinks.)

- Ask children to complete photocopiable page 23 'Dash it!' independently.

**Differentiation**

**Support:** Allow children to complete only the first part of the activity.

**Extension:** Challenge children to choose another chapter and discuss how it would be different if commas or brackets were used instead of dashes.

## 5. Semicolon independence

### Objective
To use semicolons to mark boundaries between independent clauses.

### What you need
Copies of *Stormbreaker*, photocopiable page 24 'Is it closely related?'

### What to do
- *Stormbreaker* contains many short sentences for effect, but several could have been joined to create a more flowing narrative. Briefly revise colons and full stops: colons introduce a list, dialogue, or a thought or clause that explains or follows on from the first part of the sentence (for example, 'Alex used coded message: he etched an 'A' in the corner.'); full stops mark the end of a sentence.

- Ask: *What does a semicolon do?* (It separates items in lists that may already contain commas, or separates clauses.) Focus on semicolons working with or as conjunctions/linking words separating <u>related</u> but independent clauses. The semicolon comes before a conjunction or linking word, or replaces it. Ask: *Why would you use one instead of a full stop?* (to continue a theme in compound or complex sentences, or to avoid short, choppy sentences and overuse of 'and' or 'but') However, if clauses aren't closely related, a full stop should be used.

- Ask pairs of children to complete photocopiable page 24 'Is it closely related?' Bring the class together to share and discuss their answers and increase awareness of how semicolons can be used to increase flow and variety in sentences.

### Differentiation
**Support:** Allow children to complete only the first part of the activity.

**Extension:** Children can review an extract from *Stormbreaker* to find sentences that could also be linked by semicolons.

## 6. It's perfect

### Objective
To use the perfect form of verbs.
### What you need
Prompt cards.

### What to do
- Briefly revise tenses by inviting volunteers to say sentences about Alex using the simple past, present and future.

- Now focus on perfect tenses. Explain that the perfect forms of verbs show an action has been completed, or by when it will have been completed, and sometimes why. Write these sentences on the board and invite a volunteer to explain how the perfect tenses are created using the verb 'have': 'I have learned my lesson.', 'I had learned my lesson.', 'I will have learned my lesson.' ('have' changes the tense and is combined with the key verb's past participle – present perfect: 'have'; past perfect: 'had'; future perfect: 'will have').

- Explain that adverbs or other words link the perfect verbs to a time or cause. Organise the children into groups and hand out sets of prompt cards with the following (or choose your own): *When Alex has (verb), he...; After his uncle had (verb), Alex...; When Alex had (verb), he...; By the time..., Alex will have (verb); Because Sayle had (verb), he...* Encourage the children to invent creative sentences to complete the prompts, swapping cards to try different ones. Ask a spokesperson from each group to share their best sentences with the class.

### Differentiation
**Support:** Give children completed prompt cards. Ask them to underline the perfect verbs and identify if they are past, present or future perfect.

# Spelling 'ough' is tough!

● Write each word containing the 'ough' letter string in the correct jellyfish below.

| | | | | | |
|---|---|---|---|---|---|
| ought | trough | bought | although | thought | borough |
| nought | tough | brought | thorough | fought | plough |
| wrought | through | sought | dough | cough | drought |
| rough | though | bough | hiccough | enough | |

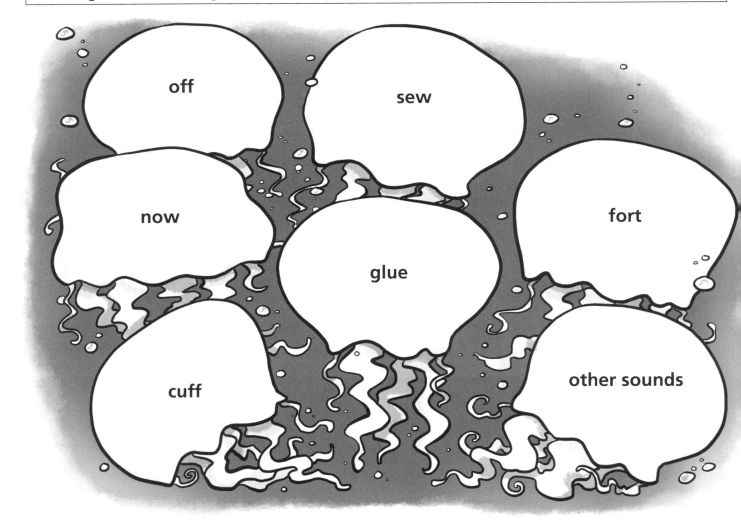

off

sew

now

glue

fort

cuff

other sounds

● Choose words containing the 'ough' letter string to use in your own sentences related to *Stormbreaker*. You can choose words from above or think of your own.

1. _____

2. _____

3. _____

4. _____

# Dash it!

- Rewrite each sentence, using one or two dashes to mark off additional information (parenthesis).

1. He couldn't allow Jack the closest thing he'd had to a mother to be sent back to America.

2. Herod Sayle admired the jellyfish the deadly Physalia Physalis.

3. "Why would my uncle who was always so careful not have worn his seatbelt that night?" mused Alex.

- Rewrite each sentence, adding additional information or an afterthought using one or two dashes.

4. Alan Blunt was not the chairman of a bank.

5. Alex knew where he'd seen the name Stryker before.

6. "Eating goat is not my favourite thing."

# Is it closely related?

● Choose which punctuation mark to add in each box below.

.?!

1. Stop sneaking around ☐ You don't know what you'll find.

2. That was terrifying ☐ I have to carry on.

3. What are you doing ☐ You're not allowed in here.

4. Alex heard a faint noise ☐ Quickly, he grabbed the map.

Full stops, question marks and exclamation marks show where sentences end;
semicolons <u>can</u> link two closely-related sentences.

● In each sentence, replace a conjunction with a semicolon.

5. He calls it spectacular but I call it creepy.

_____

6. There's a good chance you will succeed and I hope you do.

_____

7. Alex was forced to take the gadgets although he thought they were silly.

_____

● Add a semicolon to make sense of these sentences.

8. His uncle had trained him well he just hadn't realised.

9. I understand jellyfish they are outsiders like me.

10. Alex thought hard suddenly, the penny dropped!

# PLOT, CHARACTER & SETTING ▶

---

## 1. Casting a character

> **Objective**
> In writing narratives, to consider how authors have developed characters.
>
> **What you need**
> Copies of *Stormbreaker*, photocopiable page 29 'Casting brief for _____'.

### What to do

- After reading to the end of the chapter, 'So What Do You Say?', ask: *Has anyone seen the Stormbreaker film? Do the characters in the book so far match how they are in the film?* Broaden the discussion to include other films of books they have seen. *Is it better to read the book or see the film first?*

- Ask: *What would you look for when deciding who to cast as a character in a film based on a book?* (Encourage answers relating to what the character does, how they look, speak, move, and so on.) Using evidence from the first four chapters, build a class picture of Alex so far. Demonstrate how his character is built from small details and categorise the characteristics children find in the text on the board: 'how he looks', 'how he speaks', 'his actions', and so on. Ask: *Do you think you would get on with Alex? Why?*

- Give pairs of children photocopiable page 29 'Casting brief for _____'. Ask them to complete the profile for Mr Blunt, a minor but well-described character.

> **Differentiation**
> **Support:** Give the children page references to help them find useful information for the profile.
>
> **Extension:** Challenge children to do a profile for Mrs Jones.

---

## 2. Another perspective

> **Objective**
> To draw inferences, justifying them with evidence.
>
> **What you need**
> Copies of *Stormbreaker*.

### What to do

- Read the chapter 'Night Visitors' up to '"Let's eat," Sayle said', with the class following in their books. Invite a volunteer to summarise what happens before asking: *Is the story told by a limited or omniscient third-person narrator? How can you tell?* (limited – only gives Alex's thoughts and feelings; no foreshadowing) *What does Alex think of Sayle?* Encourage answers backed by evidence from the text and guide children to consider Alex's actions, thoughts and what he says.

- In small groups, ask the children to re-read the extract and discuss what Herod Sayle might be thinking about Alex. Write some questions on the board to guide their discussions: *Does Sayle believe Alex's story about why he is called Alex, not Felix? Why does Sayle want to play snooker with Alex? Why does he agree to Alex's 100-pounds-a-point challenge? What does he think when Alex snookers him? What is Sayle's mood at the end of the game?*

- Bring the class together and invite volunteers to take turns retelling the snooker game in third-person narrative, focusing on Sayle's actions, thoughts and words rather than Alex's. Start them off: 'Sayle decided to test his visitor by calling him "Felix" – supposedly accidentally.'

> **Differentiation**
> **Support:** Allow the children to retell just one or two paragraphs of the extract.
>
> **Extension:** The children can experiment with retelling the snooker game in first-person narrative from either Sayle's or Alex's point of view.

## 3. Down to the wire

### Objective
To discuss and evaluate how authors use language.

### What you need
Copies of *Stormbreaker*, thesauruses.

### What to do

- Before reading the chapter 'Death in the Long Grass', invite predictions on what might happen. Remind children that predictions, unlike guesses, are based on textual evidence. Then, ask the children to read the chapter in groups, taking turns to narrate using expression to enhance the tension and atmosphere as the chapter progresses.

- Re-read from 'It was only once he'd left' to 'the killing field'. Ask: *What happens to the sentences as Alex gets closer to danger?* (The length varies, interspersing shorter ones reflecting Alex's thoughts.) *Why is 'To the killing field.' an entire paragraph?* (It emphasises the approaching danger.)

- Focus on imagery. Ask: *How does the author describe the long grass?* ('shimmering green cage'.) A little further on, ask: *What does he liken the quad bikes to?* (wasps) *Why is this an effective image?* (It suggests an insect on the attack.)

- Ask the children to focus on words that increase the impact of the description of Alex's ordeal. In their groups, they should skim from where the quad bikes appear, jotting down descriptive or effective words. Discuss these in a plenary session. Add further words if necessary and demonstrate how descriptive verbs in particular enhance the writing.

### Differentiation
**Support:** Ask the children to identify five verbs relating to the quad bikes' sound or actions.

**Extension:** Encourage children to use a thesaurus and experiment with synonyms to see how the effect changes.

## 4. Who is Herod Sayle?

### Objective
To summarise the main ideas drawn from more than one paragraph.

### What you need
Copies of *Stormbreaker*, photocopiable page 30 'Who is Herod Sayle?'

### What to do

- Re-read the chapter 'So What Do You Say?' together, with children taking the speaking parts as you narrate. Ask: *What does the expression 'Too good to be true' mean?* (Something seems so good it makes you suspicious that it cannot be real or something is wrong with it.) *How might Sayle be 'Too good to be true'?* (Few people would give away so many free computers.) *What's your opinion?* (Encourage reasoned answers.)

- Re-read Sayle's letter to the Prime Minister and ask: *How does Sayle feel about England? What does 'cock-a-hoop' mean?* (extremely pleased, especially about a triumph or success) *If the whole Government was cock-a-hoop, why is only Blunt concerned?* (Encourage reasoned answers.)

- Ask the children to refer to the section beginning 'Herod Sayle was born…' and make notes on Sayle's life in the relevant part of photocopiable page 30, 'Who is Herod Sayle?'

- Ask pairs of children to read the chapter 'The School Bully', making notes on the photocopiable page on Sayle's version of his life. Then, using their notes, they should write a paragraph summarising why only MI6 seemed worried by Sayle's gesture to give away computers.

### Differentiation
**Support:** Provide a writing frame for the paragraph: 'Initially, the Government was not worried because…'; 'However,…'; 'This means that…'

**Extension:** Challenge children to develop their paragraphs into a report warning the Prime Minister.

# 5. The importance of Yassen

## Objective
To provide reasoned justifications for their views.

## What you need
Copies of *Stormbreaker*.

## What to do

- Explore why the author included Yassen Gregorovich, a minor character, in the story. Ask: *Who first mentions Yassen and why?* (Blunt and Mrs Jones – she thinks Alex should know Yassen probably killed Ian Rider and may be working with Sayle.) *How does Blunt respond to Mrs Jones' concern about Yassen killing Alex?* (It is not their problem – it would show something is wrong at Sayle Enterprises.) *What does this tell you about Blunt?* (He is cold-hearted, and focused on his work.) Ask: *What is a contract killer?* (someone who kills for money)

- Ask the children to skim the last four pages of 'Night Visitors' and the first three of 'Death in the Long Grass' with the following question in mind: *Why doesn't Alex alert MI6 that he has seen Sayle?* Ask: *What would you have done in Alex's position? Why?*

- Re-read the last three pages of the novel to the class. Ask: *Is Yassen an honourable person?* (Encourage reasoned answers. He could be seen as honourable for not killing Alex as a witness to his killing of Sayle.) *How important is Yassen to the plot?* (not very, until the end) In groups, ask the children to discuss why Yassen was included. Invite a spokesperson from each group to report their ideas. Remind them to consider that *Stormbreaker* is the first in a series.

## Differentiation
**Extension:** Challenge children to predict whether/how Yassen and Alex will meet again.

# 6. All is not as it seems

## Objective
To explain and discuss their understanding of what they have read.

## What you need
Copies of *Stormbreaker*.

## What to do

- As in other spy novels, many things in *Stormbreaker* are not as they appear on the surface. Divide the board into three columns, with the headings 'People', 'Places' and 'Things'. Brainstorm with the class everything that was not as it appeared at first sight, for example: Ian Rider, Royal and General offices, Blunt, gadgets, Sayle Enterprises, even Alex. Invite volunteers to choose one and explain why it was a good cover, disguise or camouflage.

- Discuss some pertinent expressions. Ask: *How is the expression, 'Never judge a book by its cover' relevant to the story?* (Appearances can be deceptive.) *Why could Sayle be described as a 'wolf in sheep's clothing'?* (His seemingly benevolent gesture was in fact malevolent.)

- Ask if anyone has heard of a 'Trojan horse'. Explain it came from the ancient Greek tale of a hollow, wooden horse secretly filled with soldiers used to deceive and conquer Troy. In computers, it refers to a seemingly harmless programme that is in fact malicious. *Why is the Stormbreaker the perfect Trojan horse?* (It is attractive, exciting new technology; it seems a generous gesture; the Prime Minister is keen to look good; it would appeal to schools and children.) Ask the children to use these reasons to write a persuasive paragraph explaining why the Stormbreaker is an ideal Trojan horse.

## Differentiation
**Support:** Provide a writing frame with linking words: 'because', 'although', 'therefore', 'finally'.

PLOT, CHARACTER & SETTING

## 7. The clock strikes 12

### Objective
To identify and discuss conventions in writing by investigating endings.

### What you need
Copies of *Stormbreaker*.

### What to do

- Ask: *What is the climax in a story?* (the turning point between rising and falling action; the most dramatic moment where conflict/problem/dilemma is confronted) Encourage children to use story-structure vocabulary in their responses.

- *What is the main problem/conflict/dilemma in Stormbreaker?* (Alex must uncover and thwart Sayle's plan.) Read the chapter 'Twelve o'clock' with the class. Ask: *What happens in Stormbreaker's climax?* (Alex crashes in to stop the Prime Minister pressing the button; Stormbreaker is destroyed.) *Why isn't this the ending?* (Sayle has disappeared; Alex hasn't spoken to MI6.) Remind the children that the narrative after the climax leading to the resolution and conclusion is known as the 'falling action'. *What is the effect of the chapter ending?* (It is a loose end, a cliffhanger, and it makes you want to read on.)

- In groups, ask the children to read the final chapter, 'Yassen', and discuss the following: *Is it a satisfying ending? Why?* Ask groups to share their opinions. Ask: *How does the ending suggest it is part of a series?* (MI6 may contact Alex again; Alex says he'll kill Yassen one day.) Invite suggestions for a different ending, for example, if Sayle had left in the helicopter and taken Alex. Ask: *How would it change the story?*

### Differentiation
**Support:** Provide a writing frame for children to give their opinion of the ending.

**Extension:** Children can write a plan for an alternative final chapter.

## 8. The sequel

### Objectives
To identify and discuss conventions in writing by exploring plot lines; to predict what might happen.

### What you need
Copies of *Stormbreaker*, photocopiable page 31 'The sequel'.

### What to do

- Ask: *What are the key features of a book review?* List them on the board (title, author, main character/s, setting, plot summary, opinion of book, recommendation, mostly present tense). Survey how many children have chosen to read a book from a review or recommendation.

- Ask the class to imagine another book in the *Alex Rider* series – a sequel. *Which significant characters would you keep? Why? Which minor characters would you bring back? Why?* (For example, Wolf, Yassen, Jack.) Ask: *What new characters could you include?* For example, the antagonist, or minor characters who may be good, bad or both (like Wolf). Encourage creativity and invite children to suggest names that reflect something about the character (Mrs Jones, for example, is an ordinary-sounding name, which is a good cover).

- Ask: *What will Alex have to do 'to save his country'?* Hand out photocopiable page 31 'The sequel' and ask pairs or small groups to write a book review of the sequel – with just enough detail, but not too much to be a spoiler.

### Differentiation
**Support:** Suggest an idea for an antagonist and a plot line, for example: Alex has to discover why schoolchildren across the country are disappearing whenever they go to the doctor.

**Extension:** Children can write an opening paragraph, a chapter, or an extract to include in the review.

# Casting brief for _____

- Use Chapters 2–4 to complete the casting brief for Mr Blunt.

Name: _____

Occupation: _____

Role in novel: _____

**Character Notes**

Physical description: _____

_____

Clothes: _____

_____

Type of voice: _____

_____

Typical dialogue/expressions: _____

_____

_____

Unusual characteristics: _____

_____

_____

_____

Adjectives to describe him:

# Who is Herod Sayle?

● Make notes on Sayle's life on the timeline. Then make notes on Sayle's version of his life. Compare the two.

**Herod Sayle's life – as seen by others**

**'My life' by Herod Sayle**

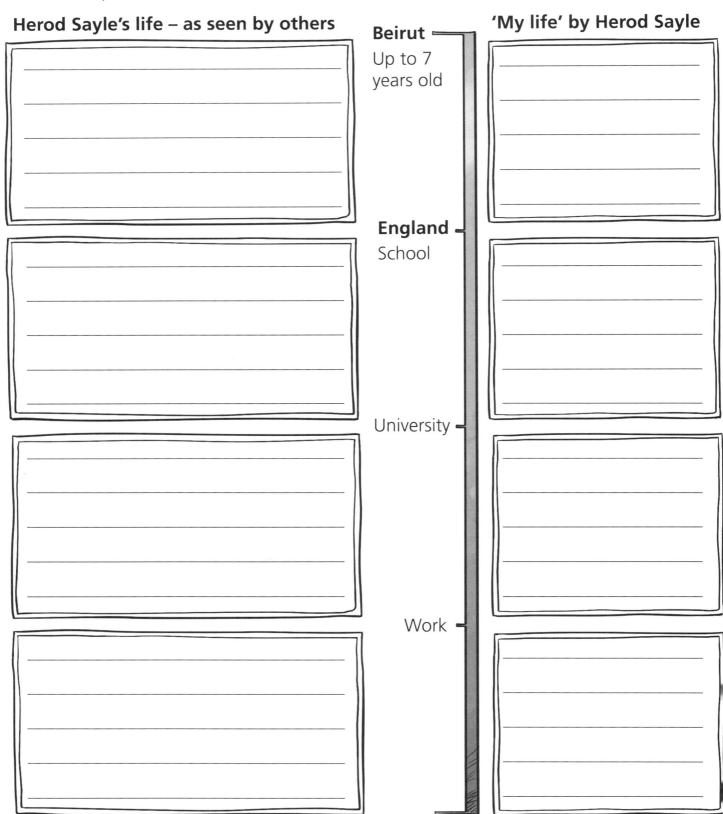

**Beirut**
Up to 7 years old

**England**
School

University

Work

# The sequel

- Write a review of your sequel to *Stormbreaker*.

**Title:** _____

**Author:** _____

**Plot:**

**Characters:**

**Opinion:**

**Recommendation:**

# TALK ABOUT IT ▶

## 1. Pleased to meet you

### Objective
To introduce a friend, focusing on speaking audibly and fluently.

### What you need
Copies of *Stormbreaker*.

### What to do

- Write the question 'Who is Alex?' on the board. Ask: *Based on the first chapter, how would you describe Alex Rider?* (Discuss first impressions: a 14-year-old boy, lives with his uncle and housekeeper, his uncle dies.) Ask: *If Alex was in your class, do you think you would be friends with him?* (Discuss children's ideas.)

- Ask pairs to brainstorm everything they've learned about Alex in the first chapter. Allow them to add additional information that they think is a likely part of his life and his character (for example, he's not a big talker, he enjoys playing computer games, he's not sentimental).

- Invite the children to imagine having Alex as a fellow classmate. Ask pairs to work together to prepare a speech introducing 'My friend, Alex'. Encourage creativity and suggest they include anecdotes and stories about what they have done with Alex or things they know he has done. They should practise presenting the speech, taking turns to speak audibly and fluently.

- Ask pairs to present to the class and encourage constructive feedback.

### Differentiation

**Support:** Suggest various speech starters other than: 'I'd like to introduce you to my friend, Alex.'

**Extension:** Challenge children to prepare an introduction of another character, such as Jack Starbright. Invite them to include additional, reasonable information to add to her character.

## 2. Toys and gadgets

### Objective
To demonstrate a spy gadget, ensuring they maintain the interest of listeners.

### What you need
Copies of *Stormbreaker*, examples of modern toys and gadgets.

### What to do

- Read the chapter 'Toys Aren't Us', from where Smithers enters until 'He waddled off...' Ask: *What was the challenge facing Smithers?* ('to think what a fourteen-year-old might carry with him – and adapt it.') *Why was it such a challenge for Smithers?* (He hadn't had to equip a boy before and found it hard to think of ideas.) *Do you carry any of these things around with you? Why?* (Encourage reasons – outdated/no longer popular.)

- Ask: *What things would a teenager carry today, apart from a mobile phone?* Encourage discussion and write children's ideas on the board. (Ideas might include: chewing gum, headphones, a beanie or scarf, lip balm, a fitness tracker, a wallet/purse, a watch.)

- The children should imagine they have been asked to help Smithers with some new ideas for gadgets to equip Alex Rider. Using examples of toys and gadgets from home, they should design three items to present to the class and describe the undercover functions of each. Encourage them to plan and prepare their presentation, including an introduction and a conclusion.

- Remind them to speak clearly and with expression when presenting.

### Differentiation

**Support:** Let children practise with a partner.

**Extension:** Challenge children to design a useful gadget for their parent/carer to use at home.

# 3. It's a secret

### Objective
To role play a conversation.

### What you need
Copies of *Stormbreaker*, photocopiable page 35 'We need to talk'.

### Cross-curricular link
Drama

## What to do

- The plot hinges on key conversations in the story. Ask children to skim through the book to identify some of these, for example: Alex's conversation with Sayle at dinner, or his conversations with Mr Blunt and Mrs Jones. List them on the board and note the characters involved.

- Ask pairs of children to create a secret telephone conversation that might have happened between two characters at any point in the story. They can choose their own scene, or one of the following: Alex reporting back to Mrs Jones while he is at Sayle Enterprises; Mrs Jones and Mr Blunt discussing their plans for Alex; Sayle and Yassen organising their getaway. Hand out photocopiable page 35 'We need to talk' and let children use it to make notes.

- Before role playing the conversation, ask the children to think of some stage rules and write them on the board (for example, face the audience when you speak, know your position, speak audibly and fluently, show expression, use body language). Let pairs practise their role play with these things in mind.

- When the children perform, encourage the audience to use the list of stage rules to note things they see in action.

### Differentiation
**Support:** Children can choose a conversation in the book and prepare a dramatic reading.

**Extension:** Challenge children to write a text-message conversation between two characters.

# 4. Don't shoot!

### Objectives
To take part in discussions; to express and justify opinions.

### What you need
Copies of *Stormbreaker*.

### Cross-curricular link
PSHE

## What to do

- The story features many violent scenes, including where guns are used and people are shot. Use this as an opportunity to discuss the issue of guns and violence. Write on the board: 'We can't give a teenager a gun'. Ask: *Who says this and in what context?* (Mr Blunt when speaking to Mrs Jones about equipping Alex for his mission) *Who agrees or disagrees with this statement?* (Ask for a show of hands, but there is no need to discuss this further at this point.)

- Alex is given useful gadgets to help him survive, but not weapons. Ask: *What were their reasons for this? Do you think this was fair? Why do you think the author did this?* Encourage discussion, allowing children to express their opinions, while monitoring the discussion sensitively.

- In small groups, ask children to discuss the argument: 'Alex should/should not be allowed to carry a gun.' They should list four or five reasons to justify each side of the argument and support their opinions.

- A spokesperson from each group should report back, followed by a whole-class discussion.

### Differentiation
**Extension:** Debate the issue of violence in the story, and whether the book is suitable for children. Choose one side of the argument: 'Books like these should/should not be banned.'

## 5. Act it out

> **Objective**
> To plan a mission, using spoken language to imagine and explore ideas.
>
> **What you need**
> Copies of *Stormbreaker*, photocopiable page 36 'Mission X'.
>
> **Cross-curricular link**
> Geography

### What to do

- Children should work in large groups so that they benefit from everyone's input and different ideas. In the chapter 'Dozmary Mine', read the list of articles that Alex buys from the maritime store in preparation for his mission. Write these on the board: 'a powerful torch', 'a jersey', 'a length of rope' and 'a box of chalk'. Discuss: *What is each item used for? How did Alex know he would need these things?*

- Ask: *When you go on holiday, how do you know what to pack?* (It depends on <u>where</u> you're going, <u>what</u> the weather will be like, <u>how</u> you will travel, <u>when</u> you will return, <u>what</u> you will be doing.) Hand out photocopiable page 36 'Mission X'. Ask groups to imagine they have been sent on a secret mission. They must decide where it will take place (for example, the desert, a jungle, a mountain, a space station, the bottom of the sea), the reason for their mission, and ten items they will need. They should arrange these ten items in order of priority. Let children explore ideas and use their imaginations to come to a solution.

- Monitor the groups, ensuring everyone participates. Let them choose a spokesperson to report back to the class.

> **Differentiation**
> **Support:** List essential items required for a spy party. Identify the five most important items.

## 6. A different perspective

> **Objective**
> To talk about ways to help others, justifying answers and opinions.
>
> **What you need**
> Copies of *Stormbreaker*, photocopiable page 37 'Helping hands'.
>
> **Cross-curricular link**
> PSHE

### What to do

- Refer to the final chapter where Alex reflects on how he feels. Read aloud from the paragraph beginning 'He should have been feeling better'. Ask: *Why is Alex unhappy?* (He was forced to help, he didn't have a choice.) *Do you think Alex would have helped to save the schoolchildren if he was given the choice?* Discuss children's ideas.

- Invite the children to reflect on times when they have helped out. Ask: *What have you done to help at home and/or in your community? How does helping out make you feel? How do you feel if you are forced to help?* Encourage discussion.

- Hand out photocopiable page 37 'Helping hands' and ask children to read through the questions together in small groups. Give them a few minutes to quietly make notes on their own, then let them take turns to share their answers.

- Guide and facilitate the discussion, ensuring everyone has a chance to participate.

> **Differentiation**
> **Support:** Invite children to think of other books and stories where one character helps another.
>
> ---
>
> **Extension:** Imagine a new rule at school: 'Everyone must help at least one person a day.' Discuss the pros and cons of this rule, and of forcing people to do this.

# We need to talk

- Choose two characters to conduct a secret phone conversation at a particular point in the story.
- Make notes to show what each character says

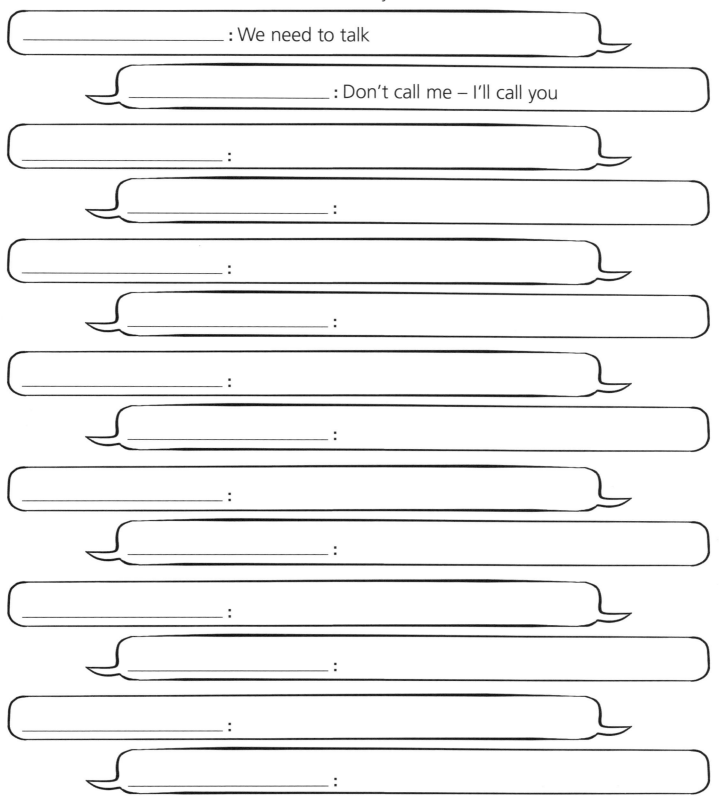

_____ : We need to talk

_____ : Don't call me – I'll call you

_____ :

_____ :

_____ :

_____ :

_____ :

_____ :

_____ :

_____ :

_____ :

_____ :

# Mission X

- Work with your group to complete this mission brief. Once you know where you are going and why, decide on the most essential items required for your mission. Good luck!

**1. Date and time of mission:** _____

**Nature and location of mission:** _____

_____

**Code names of agents in the team:** _____

_____

**Expected weather and terrain:** _____

_____

**Possible challenges:** _____

_____

**2. List ten essential items. Number them in order of priority.**

| Essential item | Priority |
| --- | --- |
| • | |
| • | |
| • | |
| • | |
| • | |
| • | |
| • | |
| • | |
| • | |
| • | |

# Helping hands

- Make notes on the following questions.
- In groups, discuss each question. Everyone should have a turn to give their answer.

**1.** Does Alex help by choice or because he has to? Explain why.

_____

_____

**2.** How does Alex feel about helping?

_____

_____

**3.** Do you think Alex is glad he helped in the end?

_____

_____

**4.** Do you help by choice or because you have to?

_____

_____

**5.** How do you feel when you are forced to help?

_____

_____

**6.** What sort of help are you asked to give?

_____

_____

# GET WRITING ▶

## 1. Tribute to Ian Rider

### Objective

To write a tribute, identifying the audience for and purpose of the writing.

### What you need

Copies of *Stormbreaker*, examples of tributes (of famous people), photocopiable page 41 'My tribute to Ian Rider'.

### Cross-curricular link

PSHE

### What to do

- Focus on the first chapter. Read Alex's thoughts after hearing that his uncle, Ian Rider, has died. Read from 'Alex thought of the man...' to 'It was only a thumbnail sketch'. Ask: *How well did Alex know his uncle? Did they have a good relationship?*

- If possible, read out some examples of tributes and discuss their features. Ask: *What is a tribute?* (something you say or do to honour someone you respect, admire or love, usually when someone has died) *What style is it?* (formal but personal) *What tense is it in?* (mostly past tense)

- Hand out photocopiable page 41 'Tribute to Ian Rider'. Children should gather details about Ian from the first few chapters of the story, to help them with their tribute. Remind them to consider clues such as the photograph on Rider's desk showing them on adventurous holidays together. Importantly, remind them that Alex's tribute should not divulge Ian's secret identity as a spy!

- Children should use their notes to plan, draft and edit a personal tribute. Invite volunteers to read their tributes out to the class.

### Differentiation

**Support:** Provide paragraph starters for the children for each section of the tribute.

**Extension:** Let the children prepare and present their tribute as a speech.

## 2. Reviewing books

### Objectives

To note and develop initial ideas; to design a questionnaire for a would-be spy, identifying the audience for and purpose of the writing.

### What you need

Copies of *Stormbreaker*.

### Cross-curricular link

PSHE

### What to do

- Write 'SPY' on the board, and the following headings underneath: 'Age', 'Skills', 'Qualities', 'Connections', 'Previous Experience'. Ask: *In the story, what types of people did MI6 need?* (Discuss spy qualities mentioned in the story and from prior knowledge.)

- Ask pairs of children to make notes about Alex, identifying the things that equipped him to be an MI6 spy. Let them skim the story (especially Chapters 4–6 and Chapter 10) to remind them of some examples: he doesn't have parents, he's learned to climb and dive, he's lived abroad, he's a karate expert, he's brave and resourceful, he's an expert on a quad bike. Together, share ideas and opinions about Alex's spy qualities.

- Invite children to imagine that Alex had to apply for the job of an MI6 spy. Explain that their task is to design a questionnaire to ascertain whether Alex is the right person for the job. Discuss different types of questions they could ask. Encourage them to pay attention to the format and organisation of the text.

- Ask pairs to swap questionnaires and complete each other's, as if they are Alex.

### Differentiation

**Extension:** Challenge children to design a form for a competition to visit Sayle Enterprises, like the one mentioned in Chapter 4. They should complete it as Felix Lester.

# 3. What is weird?

## Objective
To create a factfile, using organisational and presentational devices.

## What you need
Copies of *Stormbreaker* and Extract 4.

## What to do

- Hand out copies of Extract 4 and invite the children to skim it. Ask: *How can you tell that this is a non-fiction text?* (the heading, layout, the use of bullet points, the inclusion of a labelled diagram) Invite them to use a coloured marker to highlight the facts. *What do you notice?* (There are mainly facts.)

- Turn to the chapter 'Physalia Physalis' and read aloud the description of the car at the start of the chapter. Ask the children to identify the facts and list them on the board. Ask: *How would you change the text to look like a factfile?* (Remove the narrative style and all opinions; change the layout to include a labelled diagram, bullet points and a heading, with subheadings covering aspects such as model, manufacturer, colour, interior, engine, price.) Let children discuss the question in pairs, then share ideas as a class.

- Now turn to 'Dozmary Mine'. Let children work together to extract facts about the mine. They should then plan, write and edit a factfile about the mine. Provide ideas for subheadings, such as 'Location', 'Type of mine', 'History', 'Present-day owners and access'.

- Display children's factfiles.

## Differentiation

**Support:** Let children do a factfile for the Stormbreaker instead of the mine.

**Extension:** Challenge children to create a factfile on a different dangerous sea creature that Sayle might have kept in his tank.

# 4. Write the script

## Objectives
To write a mini-script, considering setting and character; to perform their own compositions.

## What you need
Copies of *Stormbreaker*, an example of a script, photocopiable page 42 'The script'.

## Cross-curricular link
Drama

## What to do

- Organise the children into small groups. Assign one story chapter to each group. Ask the children to identify a key conversation in their chapter and to prepare a dramatic reading.

- Ask: *To act out these scenes, would you use the book?* (no, actors use scripts) *How is a script different from a book?* (As well as lines, a script gives the actor and stage hands instructions on what props to use, where actors must stand and what they must do on stage.)

- Show an example of a script and ask the children to identify features such as scene title and brief scene description; characters' names on the left (followed by a colon); new line for each new speaker; stage directions in brackets and italics before or after a character speaks; stage directions in present tense describing how actors must speak and move; no speech marks; punctuation emphasising expression and pauses. Write the features on the board as a checklist.

- Hand out photocopiable page 42 'The script'. In their groups, children should choose a scene and turn it into a mini-script. When they have checked and edited their work, ask them to present it to the class.

## Differentiation

**Extension:** Let children swap scripts and act out a scene written by another group.

# ▼ GET WRITING

## 5. Check this out!

> ### Objective
> To design an advertisement, choosing vocabulary, grammar and punctuation to enhance meaning.
>
> ### What you need
> Copies of *Stormbreaker*, thesauruses, examples of advertisements.

### What to do

- Ask the children to identify chapters in the story where the Stormbreaker computer is described. List these chapters on the board. In pairs, invite the children to skim these chapters and note all the features of the Stormbreaker. Identify interesting vocabulary used to describe it (for example 'revolutionary', 'state-of-the-art', 'round processor', 'brings subjects to life', and so on.)

- Let the children use thesauruses to explore other words to describe the computer and what it does. Note them down on a mind map. Remind them to use words in their correct context.

- Display examples of adverts and ask the children to identify textual features (visually appealing, bold statements, easy-to-read font, facts and opinions combined, interesting punctuation and grammar). Discuss audience and purpose: how adverts target particular markets in order to promote and sell a product.

- In their pairs, children should discuss ideas for a poster to advertise the Stormbreaker to children in their school. Remind them to consider audience, layout, font size, vocabulary, grammar and punctuation to create the desired effect. Allow children time to plan, create, edit and complete their adverts on poster paper, and display them.

> ### Differentiation
> **Support:** Children can use computers to design and print their advertisements.
> _____
> **Extension:** Children can create an advertisement for one of the gadgets that Smithers presents to Alex.

## 6. Read all about it

> ### Objective
> To write a news report, identifying the purpose of the writing and selecting the appropriate form.
>
> ### What you need
> Copies of *Stormbreaker*, photocopiable page 43 'Read all about it'.
>
> ### Cross-curricular links
> History, geography, PSHE

### What to do

- Refer to the final two chapters where reporters witness everything but are banned from reporting the truth. In the final chapter, read from 'You might like to know about the clearing-up operation' to 'It was very close'. Ask: *Why are the reporters not allowed to report what happened?* (MI6 need to cover up the operation.) *What are they told to report?* (that Sayle was attacked by an unknown terrorist group and fled into hiding)

- Hand out photocopiable page 43 'Read all about it'. In small groups, invite the children to brainstorm the real facts of the story using question words: 'who', 'what', 'where', 'when', 'why' and 'how'. Ensure they are familiar with the difference between a fact and an opinion.

- Individually, children should use their plan to write a news report describing what actually happened that day. They should use formal language, past tense and include at least one quote from an eyewitness or person in charge. Let children read their completed reports to the class. Discuss how they may be different, yet all include the same facts.

> ### Differentiation
> **Support:** Children can focus on the lead paragraph only, including at least five important facts.
> _____
> **Extension:** Children can design a news report checklist to help them edit their work.

 # Tribute to Ian Rider

- Imagine you are Alex Rider. Make notes of the things you remember about Ian Rider and how you felt about him.
- Use your notes to write a personal tribute

---

### Tribute notes on Ian Rider

Who he was to me:

_____

_____

_____

How long we knew each other:

_____

_____

_____

Things we shared and did together:

_____

_____

_____

A particular story I will
always remember:

_____

_____

_____

His best qualities:

_____

_____

_____

What I will miss about him:

_____

_____

_____

_____

The last time I saw him:

_____

_____

_____

Our last holiday together:

_____

_____

_____

# The script

- Choose a scene in the story. Where does it take place? Which characters are involved? Imagine acting it out...
- Use this template to write a short script for your scene.

**Scene title:** _____

**Set the scene:** (Describe the setting) _____

_____

_____

**Characters:** _____

_____

**The script:**

_____    _____

_____    _____

_____    _____

_____    _____

_____    _____

_____    _____

_____    _____

_____    _____

_____    _____

_____    _____

_____    _____

# Read all about it

- Gather your facts and plan a news report on the real story.
- Eyewitness accounts often include personal opinion but as a reporter you should stick to the facts.

**Catchy headline options:**

_____

_____

**Lead paragraph facts: Who? What? When? Where?**

_____

_____

_____

**Details about the 'Why?' and 'How?':**

_____

_____

_____

_____

**Extra information and eyewitness accounts and quotes:**

_____

_____

_____

_____

We were all watching the Prime Minister, when suddenly we heard...

There was this young boy, hanging from the roof with a gun...

I heard someone shout 'Don't shoot!' and security were everywhere...

# ASSESSMENT ▶

## 1. Read aloud

> **Objectives**
> To speak audibly and fluently
>
> **What you need**
> Copies of *Stormbreaker*.

### What to do

- Explain that you will be reading aloud from *Stormbreaker*. Begin reading in a dull, slow, soft voice. Complete a paragraph then ask the children if they enjoyed listening. Ask: *How does reading aloud affect comprehension?* (How a text is read aloud affects how well the reader and the listener understand it.) Discuss the importance of reading with expression and clarity.

- Arrange children into small groups, with copies of the book. Provide a page reference and invite them to take turns reading a passage from the story, with no preparation. Afterwards, discuss how they felt about this, whether they found it difficult or easy and why.

- Ask pairs of children to practise a prepared reading of a favourite extract from the story. Write the following on the board: 'accuracy', 'fluency', 'pronunciation', 'clarity' and 'expression'. Explain and discuss each term so children understand what will be assessed. Allow time to practise with a partner and encourage them to offer feedback to each other.

- Allow all children the chance to read their extract aloud to the class.

> **Differentiation**
>
> **Support:** Vary the length of the passage to be read according to individual reading levels.
>
> **Extension:** Invite children to read aloud to a different audience and for a different purpose.

## 2. Analysing clues

> **Objective**
> To ask relevant questions.
>
> **What you need**
> Copies of *Stormbreaker*.

### What to do

- A good spy is observant! Alex Rider notices things around him and he asks questions. Look at the first three chapters of the story and ask children to find examples of where Alex questions things he sees and hears. Ask: *What questions does he ask? How do questions help Alex become a good spy?* (Questions lead to answers – good questions encourage good answers.)

- Remind the children that there are different types of question: contextual questions refer directly to information in the text, inferential questions require a deeper understanding and interpretation of the text, other questions may require the reader's opinion based on the text.

- Turn to 'Behind the Door'. Invite the children to read the chapter together. While reading, they should make notes of good question opportunities. They should consider the types of question they might ask in that situation, if they were Alex. Draw their attention to the things he observes and notices around him.

- Individually, children should design ten questions based on what Alex sees behind the door. Encourage a range of questions. Ask children to present their questions to their group and invite possible answers.

> **Differentiation**
>
> **Support:** Display question starters on the board: 'I wonder if...?', 'Could it be...?', 'What does it mean...?'
>
> **Extension:** Let children swap their questions with a partner and write possible answers.

# 3. Describe it

## Objective
To discuss the use of adjectives, understanding how these can enhance meaning.

## What you need
Copies of *Stormbreaker* and Extracts 1–3.

## What to do

- Hand out Extracts 1, 2 or 3 to small groups of children and ask them to highlight the adjectives in their extract. Invite a member of each group to read the extract aloud, omitting the highlighted words. Ask: *Which version do you prefer? How did it sound once you removed the adjectives?* Encourage reasoned answers.

- Turn to the chapter 'So What Do You Say?' and read aloud from the beginning up to 'Alex…It's good of you to join us.' Before reading, ask the children to listen out for adjectives. Afterwards, ask them for any adjectives they heard, and write them on the board.

- Discuss the difference between normal adjectives and proper adjectives and highlight examples from the text: 'Gap combat trousers', 'Nike sweatshirt', 'Asian woman', 'American tourists'. Ask: *Why do you think the author uses proper adjectives?* (So readers can understand the context; it may have something to do with advertising – invite discussion.)

- Write two separate lists of proper adjectives and nouns on the board. Ask children to match the correct adjectives to the nouns in their notebooks. For example: Italian shoes, French bread, Adidas cap, Swiss chocolate.

## Differentiation
**Support:** Children can find other examples of proper adjectives in the story.

**Extension:** Challenge children to make a 'Wanted' poster for a character. They should use adjectives effectively and include proper adjectives where appropriate.

# 4. How to…

## Objective
To write clear instructions, using organisational and presentational devices to structure the text.

## What you need
Copies of *Stormbreaker*.

## Cross-curricular link
Science

## What to do

- In the chapter 'Toys Aren't Us', read from 'I have something that might cheer you up,' to 'Thank you, Smithers'. This is where Smithers demonstrates how the spy gadgets work. Ask: *What do you think of Smithers' instructions? Where does Alex use these gadgets?* (Allow children time to skim and scan through the book before inviting volunteers to read aloud the parts where Alex uses them.) *How does he know what to do? Do you think Smithers should have included written instructions?* Discuss children's thoughts and ideas.

- Discuss the importance of clear instructions, particularly written ones. *What should instructions look and sound like?* Write children's answers on the board (clear, concise, ordered, correct spelling, punctuation and grammar, adverbials, age-appropriate, and so on).

- Working with a partner, children should choose a gadget from the story and discuss five or six clear steps explaining how to use it. Encourage them to use adverbials of time and number to link the steps and build cohesion and flow ('To begin…', 'Secondly…', 'Next…', 'Finally…').

- Then, individually, children should write their own set of instructions for using the gadget. Let them edit their work and write it out, including an appropriate heading.

## Differentiation
**Support:** Assist with the layout and provide sentence starters for four or five steps.

**Extension:** Challenge children to invent a gadget and write a set of instructions on how to use it.

# 5. Dictionary delve

## Objectives
To use a dictionary to check meaning in context; to use a thesaurus.

## What you need
Copies of *Stormbreaker*, dictionaries, thesauruses, photocopiable page 47 'Dictionary delve'.

## What to do
- Hand out dictionaries and thesauruses. Let children work individually, in pairs or in small groups. Write the following on the board: 'channel', 'choke', 'chance', 'chatter'. Revise alphabetical order (when words begin with the same first letter, go to the second, third or fourth letter to check the order). Demonstrate this on the board. Conduct a 'dictionary dash' to see who can find the words first.

- Ask the children to read the definitions aloud and discuss the various meanings and contexts. Point out that words can be nouns, verbs or adjectives according to how they are used in a sentence. Invite children to create sentences using the words in different contexts. Then ask them to suggest synonyms for these words, using a thesaurus if necessary.

- Hand out photocopiable page 47 'Dictionary delve'. Read through the instructions and the sentences, and ask children to complete it individually.

- As a class, discuss other ways to use the words in context.

### Differentiation
**Support:** Provide words from the story for the children to put into alphabetical order. Use dictionaries to find meanings and word classes. Use thesauruses to find synonyms.

**Extension:** Ask the children to find words in the story that can have different meanings.

# 6. Dear Alex

## Objective
To write an informal letter, identifying the purpose of the writing and selecting the appropriate form.

## What you need
Copies of *Stormbreaker*.

## What to do
- Ask: *Have you received or written a letter recently?* Discuss how forms of communication have changed. *In what situations would you send or receive a letter today? Is it likely to be a formal or an informal letter?* Refer to the letter in the chapter 'So What Do You Say?' Ask: *Is it formal or informal?* (formal)

- In the chapter 'Looking for Trouble', Alex discovers a note left by his uncle. Ask: *Who is it addressed to?* (There are no names on the note; he did not want to identify himself or anyone else.) *How does Alex know it is from Ian Rider?* (He recognises the handwriting.)

- Children should imagine that Ian Rider left a personal letter for Alex along with the map, knowing he might not make it out alive. *What might Ian Rider have wanted Alex to know?* Discuss the style (informal), the purpose (urgent, secret message) and a possible introduction and conclusion. Encourage creativity in expressing intrigue and mystery!

- Discuss important features of informal letter-writing and write them on the board. This should guide children as they plan, draft and edit their letters.

### Differentiation
**Support:** Provide a writing frame and paragraph starters for each section of the letter: 'Dear Alex... If you are reading this, you are in great danger!'

**Extension:** Let children design an editing checklist to use while they work.

# Dictionary delve

- Use a dictionary to find the word class of the words in bold.
- Use a thesaurus to find synonyms.

| | Word class | Synonyms |
|---|---|---|
| Alex is a 14-year-old **kid**. | | |
| He did not **kid** around. | | |
| Jack was always there to **help** around the house. | | |
| Jack was Ian Rider's hired **help**. | | |
| The **bug** was taped behind the picture. | | |
| Alex did not want to **bug** Mrs Jones or Mr Blunt. | | |
| Alex arrived at the Sayle **complex**. | | |
| It was a **complex** problem for MI6 to solve. | | |
| His **trainers** were his only protection. | | |
| At the camp, he met his **trainers**. | | |
| The last **rendezvous** point was close. | | |
| They planned to **rendezvous** that evening. | | |
| He had to **tunnel** his way through the mine. | | |
| He had a map of the **tunnel**. | | |

# SCHOLASTIC

# Available in this series:

978-1407-16055-9

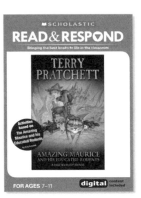

978-1407-16056-6

978-1407-16057-3

978-1407-16058-0

978-1407-16059-7

978-1407-16060-3

978-1407-16061-0

978-1407-16062-7

978-1407-16063-4

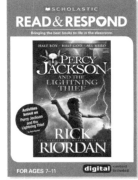

978-1407-16064-1

978-1407-16065-8

978-1407-16052-8

978-1407-16067-2

978-1407-16068-9

978-1407-16069-6

978-1407-16070-2

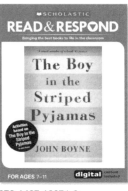

978-1407-16071-9

978-1407-17616-1

978-1407-17614-7

978-1407-17615-4

## To find out more, call:  0845 6039091
### or visit our website www.scholastic.co.uk/readandrespond